"Bookstores are filled with stories that tell you how to be rich. *The Millionaire Mentor* goes far beyond that. It shares the secrets of fulfilling life's ultimate dream—discovering one's PASSION." **—William A. Welsome, Founder & CEO, Wealth Capital Corporation**

"Greg Reid is a gifted storyteller who knows what he's talking about. *The Millionaire Mentor* is based on real life success strategies that actually work. The bottom line is that these are not just ideas and theories he's throwing out. The story reveals the actual steps we each need to take to become a great success." **—Mary Gale Hinrichsen, Ph.D.**

"*The Millionaire Mentor* is a must read for people who want to excel in sales or business. On page 41, make sure you read Step #5, 'The Warm Down.' This is the big key to building a repeat business that most people miss."

—Tom "Big Al" Schreiter, Publisher, FortuneNow.com

"*The Millionaire Mentor* is absolutely amazing! I love it. A lovely story and so true—so real and wise. Both beginners and seasoned entrepreneurs will find something new that they don't know or realize. Those wishing to succeed, discover their purpose, and enjoy their lives need to read it." **—Irena Whitfield, Internet Business Consultant for 3rdMillennium, theCassiopeia.com**

"Love your book. It could become a classic like *The Richest Man in Babylon*. You have wrapped a good package around the ideas of great thinkers, leaders, and salespeople. I felt the influence of Lincoln and some of today's bestselling authors and speakers. I could picture myself when you discussed the people out to kill your dreams and the importance of finding positive people to support you." **—Donald L. Peters, Iwillsellyourstuff.com**

"*The Millionaire Mentor* is a high-octane, turbocharged tool for the serious student of success. Greg Reid has blended years of solid, practical field-tested business and personal development principles into an easy-to-read inspirational story that works! Get it, read it, discuss it, live it, teach it… and reap the benefits now."

—David Corbin, Author of *Psyched on Service: Building a Total Service Mentality*

"*The Millionaire Mentor* is a Winner! This easy-to-read Parable can remind even the most seasoned professional just how simple it can be to achieve extraordinary success while making a positive impact on other people's lives."

—Phil Wexler, Author, *Non-Manipulative Selling*

"Greg Reid catches his readers' attention with this inspirational future classic, *The Millionaire Mentor*. Read this book, and you'll have an easy-to-follow blueprint to financial success."

—Harry Paul, Bestselling Co-Author of *Fish!*

The
Millionaire Mentor

GREG S. REID

Copyright © 2004 by Greg S. Reid
ISBN 0-938716-49-2
Special Edition

Published by
Possibility Press

5   6   7   8   9   10

Publisher's Cataloging-in-Publication
(Provided by Quality Books, Inc.)

Reid, Greg S.
    The millionaire mentor : a simple way to get ahead in your work and in life / Greg S. Reid.
    p. cm.
    "The truly rich have hearts of gold."
    LCCN 2003107028
    ISBN 0-938716-49-2 (paper)

    1. Success.   I. Title.

BF637.S8R385 2003   646.7
                      QB103-200437

Manufactured in the United States of America

Top Mentors and Leaders Share Early Praise for...
The Millionaire Mentor
by Greg S. Reid

"The Millionaire Mentor is undoubtedly one of the most unique, insightful, and useful 'how-to' books to come along in quite some time. The book's message is big, the story powerful, and the impact positively life-changing."

—Linda Forsythe, Publisher, *Mentors Magazine*

"Everybody can benefit from a mentor, either an individual or group. Many CEOs in our club have belonged to Presidential Advisory Councils for decades, and claim it is the single biggest help in running a growing business. *The Millionaire Mentor* shows us how to do it."

—Joe Mancuso, CEO, Chief Executive Officers Club, Inc.

"The Millionaire Mentor is awesome. For those who are serious about having more, doing more, and being more, this book can help you tremendously. If you are looking to change your results and do so quickly, then read this book. Buy copies for those you love. They will thank you for a long time. I really respect Greg Reid and his desire to help. What a great book. Powerful!"

—Gerry Robert, Bestselling Author, *The Millionaire Mindset*

"A parable that delivers, with real-world examples anyone can relate to. A must read for all leaders, managers, coaches, colleagues, and others who work closely with those they care to excel."

—Peter Chiaramonte, Ph.D., "Coach to the World's Olympic Coaches"

"Greg, you have finally done it! You have created the hit of the year with *The Millionaire Mentor*—a simple, easy-to-read parable that really delivers. The message is both captivating and enlightening, while reaffirming the essentials of success. It is a classic in the making—sure to inspire millions."

—Eric Lofholm, Author, Speaker & Sales Trainer

"The Millionaire Mentor is destined to be a classic. It is a must read for anyone becoming a mentor. The Success Cards add an invaluable tool to the support process."

—Jim Parker, President, The Mentor Connection, Inc.

"The Millionaire Mentor is the first and only book I have read that demonstrates the absolute necessity and power of mentoring. Your life and outlook will forever be impacted by reading it."

—Philippe Matthews, Host, The Philippe Matthews Show, CEO/EmpowerMag.com

"The title could well be *The Trillionaire Mentor*. It's jam-packed with inspiration and wisdom anyone can use to truly move ahead in the best possible way."

—Charlie "Tremendous" Jones, Speaker & Bestselling Author, *Life Is Tremendous*

Dedication

To all who have made a positive impact on the lives of others—mentors, parents, coaches, teachers, and dreamers.

Acknowledgment

This book is a compilation of stories derived from personal experience. The people and characters are based on those who have touched my life. I offer my thanks to each of you by putting these teachings on paper and sharing them with others so they may learn from them.

A special note of appreciation goes to God, for with Him all things are possible.

In addition, I would like to acknowledge my presubmission editor, Pam Perry. She has given me much more than I could ever have asked by going the extra mile in offering her guidance, support, but most of all...her friendship.

Also, thank you Possibility Press for believing in me, sharing my passion, and for your creative and editorial work.

What a Message!

With *The Millionaire Mentor,* Greg Reid gives us a straightforward, illuminating, and poignant message. A master storyteller, Greg reaches out to his readers like a friend. His positive approach to work and life, as well as his sense of humor, shine through in this simple, yet profound, story. It features a professional entrepreneur and a young protégé seeking to emulate his mentor. This extraordinary parable is sure to strike a chord with anyone who has ever asked, "How can I get more out of life?"

"True wealth comes in the giving, not the keeping."

—Greg S. Reid

Contents

"Where could you be tomorrow if you put your ideas into action today?"

—Greg S. Reid

The First Meeting

It's 10 a.m. Saturday morning outside the local ice-cream parlor in small-town, U.S.A. A young man named Oscar excitedly awaits his first meeting with his new mentor. Being raised by his mother, a single parent, Oscar looks forward to spending time with a positive, supportive male role model.

Little does he know that the person he is about to meet will change his life forever.

Oscar is not a bad kid. He is what the local mentoring program considers an "at-risk" youth. Without the loving attention and encouraging influence he needs at this early time in his life, he may get sucked into a rough and tumble "street" education. This could possibly happen through the acceptance he would feel as a member of a gang, rather than from a role model who could mold his young character in a more positive manner.

The program where his mother has placed him is the talk of the town. Everyone's buzzing about the quality of the people that the organization attracts, and the extensive background checks they perform. Having met the mentor, Roy, in person, Oscar's mother knows her son is in great hands.

Oscar stands there in his t-shirt with "Hot Shot" printed on the front, watching every passing car with anticipation that the next one will bring his new friend.

The young man's eyes light up as he watches a brand new Mercedes Benz, glistening in the sunlight, roll up and stop right in front of him. The window rolls down with the touch of a switch, and a kindly looking older man says, in a friendly voice, "You must be Oscar, the young man I have an appointment with."

The boy watches, wide-eyed, as the man gets out of the car. "I'm Roy," he volunteers. Oscar is too dumbfounded to acknowledge the introduction.

"Wow!" the boy says. "You must be rich. How did you get that way?"

"Just the fact that you asked me that question means chances are one day you'll be rich too," the older man says with a grin.

"I want to be rich," the boy answers smiling. "What do I do first?"

"The real question is, what do you do *last*?" Roy says.

"Last?" Oscar asks, amazed.

"Yes," continues the mentor, in a warm and friendly tone. "Success is all about following through and taking action on your ideas. You see, most people work hard. They're excited by wonderful ideas with great potential. However, very few actually follow through on their ideas with any sort of sustained effort."

"I have an idea!" Oscar exclaims.

"That's great! Are you willing to do what it takes to make it a reality?"

"I sure am!" Oscar replies. "I don't know a lot about business, but I have an idea I'd look mighty good in that car of yours!"

The businessman holds back a smile and asks Oscar, "Do you know why most people don't follow through on their ideas?"

The boy shrugs.

"FEAR, plain and simple. And it's usually because we're afraid of one of two things—fear of success or fear of failure. There is only one way I know of to conquer one's fears and that is to meet them HEAD ON and work through the doubts."

The businessman reaches into his vest pocket, pulls out a card, and hands it to the boy, saying "You see, son, if you believe it, you CAN achieve it. Just keep taking steps toward your goals. The boy looks down at the card and reads it.

Dreams are realities on which you haven't yet taken ACTION.

"I get it!" the lad exclaims. "The first thing is to know what I'm going to do. But the main thing is to actually go out and do it."

"Keep going," Roy urges.

"My friend, Marcos, thought of this cool way to put baseball cards in bicycle spokes to make a neat sound. I gave him my allowance to do it to my bike. It's great! He said he was going to do it for every kid in school, but he never did. He could have made, like, fifty bucks!"

"Exactly! Marcos had a great idea, and even a plan, but he lacked the most important ingredient: action. The only difference between success and failure is putting the fear of 'attempt' away and actually following through," the older man patiently explains.

"Your friend was probably all excited at the thought of his dream," Roy shares, "but after thinking about it for a while, he began to doubt himself. Could he get enough cards to do all the bikes? Maybe the other kids would poke fun at him and think the whole idea was stupid. What if the cards fell out? And so on…."

"That's the fear talk that tells us all the reasons why we'll fail," the businessman continues. "Why the project's too hard, or why it won't work. Rather than turning this dream-stealing voice off, most people give in to it, instead of doing what successful people do, and that's…."

The businessman reaches into his pocket again and hands the young man another card.

<u>NEVER GIVE UP</u>!
The only two times you
need to keep pushing
on are:

When you want to and when you don't!

"Oscar, it looks as though we have a situation here."

"What do you mean?" Oscar asks, looking a little alarmed.

"Well, we could either stand outside this ice cream shop talking business, or we could go inside and continue over a sundae."

Oscar's eyes light up at the proposition. The two enter the *Palace of Frozen Delights*, and sit in a booth near the door.

"Let me tell you how this mentoring program works," Roy begins. "If you promise to diligently pursue your dreams, I'll meet you here once a month to answer any questions you have about how to reach your goals. Be sure to give your questions careful thought, and I'll do my best to lead you in the right direction."

"You'll really do that?" Oscar asks, amazed.

"Of course. If, in return, you promise to do something for me."

"What could I do for YOU?" Oscar asked, surprised, implying there would be NOTHING he could give to the man in exchange.

"All I ask is that, when you get older, you share the lessons I'm going to teach you with someone else. Do we have a deal?"

An ear-to-ear smile breaks out on the boy's face as his new mentor reaches across their desserts to shake hands on the agreement.

"Deal," Oscar says shyly, looking away.

"Great! Now grasp my hand hard, look me in the eye, and say it like you mean it!" his advisor chides.

The boy makes eye contact with the man. With strength in his tone and grip, he says, "Deal!"

"Congratulations! You've just learned your first lesson," the businessman says.

"I did?"

"You sure did. ALL good business relationships need to begin with a firm handshake and both parties happy about the terms of the contract. The agreement could be in writing or just a verbal mutual understanding, like we have."

Oscar reaches into his own pocket and offers his new friend a treasure he'd been saving for himself.

"What's this?" his advisor asks.

"It's my Barry Bonds rookie baseball card. It's the BEST one I have. I'd NEVER put it in my spokes."

"This is for *me*?" Roy asks with a smile.

"Yes," Oscar tells him with obvious pleasure. "You've given me TWO cards already, so I still owe you one."

"Thank you, Oscar," the businessman says, rising from the table. "You know young man, our arrangement may turn out even better than I'd anticipated. It seems to me you already have the personality traits that make a great leader."

"Who, me?" the boy asks in amazement.

"Yes, you." Reaching into his wallet to pay the check and leave a two-dollar tip, the businessman pulls out another card and hands it to the boy, saying, "This is my best card, given to me when I was about your age by someone who taught me what it means to be successful. See you here next month."

As the businessman walks out the door, the boy turns the card over and reads it aloud.

Our most valuable
possession is
the one that
possesses
us to
share.

Months go by, then years. The boy and the businessman have made a connection that will last a lifetime. Every month, on the same day, in the same booth, at their special meeting place, the pair exchange stories of their successes and setbacks. As the boy grows, his skills are sharpened by the old man's wisdom.

Then one night, during this adventure-filled span of time—as Oscar lies awake organizing his thoughts—an inspiration hits him like a light bulb flashing in his mind. "I think I'm ready," he whispers to himself. "Tomorrow I'm going to get my first job."

The businessman is already sitting in their booth when Oscar pulls up the next day on his battered old ten-speed bike.

"Hi, Roy! I think I'm ready for my first job!" Oscar says with glee as he bursts into the ice cream shop and plops down into his seat. "The only problem is I don't know what I can do. I'm only 13. Who's going to hire me during the summer?"

"I have an idea," the mentor says. "After we finish here, let's go for a little ride."

The boy's eyes light up at the supportive tone in his mentor's voice, anticipating what lies ahead.

Once the two have finished catching up, they walk out of the ice cream shop and get into Roy's Mercedes. They drive a few blocks to one of the local discount stores, go inside, and browse until they come to the bicycle department, where they pause.

"Go ahead, pick out your new bike," The businessman suggests.

"What are you talking about?" Oscar asks. "I don't have any money. I mean, I don't even have a job yet. Remember?"

"Don't focus on that right now," Roy tells him. "Take all the time you need, and be sure to choose the one you really want."

Roy doesn't have to twist his arm too long. With the help of a salesperson, pointing out the features, Oscar jumps on and tries out every bike in the store.

"This is it!" the boy exclaims, showing off his selection like any good TV game-show host.

"Great. It's yours," says the mentor.

"Huh?" Oscar questions. "I told you, I can't afford it. I don't even have a job yet. I wish I could buy this bike, but I can't."

"Well, I guess you'd better put it back then," Roy responds.

Oscar looks more confused than ever, and his advisor continues, "Let me tell you a quick story about a man named Henry Ford. You've heard of the Ford Motor Company, right?"

Oscar nods, "Yes."

"Mr. Ford wanted a lighter engine for his cars. So, he went to his development team and requested that they design one for the new line of cars he wanted to bring out. As the project deadline approached, the team was still stumped. They had tried and failed at every attempt to create the new engine.

They just couldn't get it to work. They told Henry Ford about their dilemma and got a response that made automotive history."

"What did he say?" the boy asks, sitting on the nicest bike in the store.

"He looked at them straight on, and in a serious tone of voice said, 'If you think you can, or you think you can't, you're right.' He then gave them a three-month deadline to figure it out."

"What happened?" the boy asks eagerly.

"Two months later, Ford's team designed and built the first V-8 engine cast in a single block."

"Wow!" The boy sighs, reassured. "Okay then. If they could do it, so can I! This is the bike I'm going to own."

"Now THAT'S what I like to hear," the businessman says with a smile.

"What can I do to get it? Like, what's the first step?" questions Oscar.

"You've already taken it," Roy answers, sounding pleased. "The first step is to decide on the goal. In this case, it's picking out the bike you want. After you decide, the best way to make your dream a reality is to break it down into baby-step goals. Here." He hands the boy another of his "famous" cards—one he had hidden in his back pocket.

Before you can even hope to reach a goal, you first need to HAVE one.

"See," the mentor continues, "all you need to do is give yourself a goal to reach, then you'll find a way to achieve it. Without a goal, what reason would you have for doing anything?"

"But what can I do to earn this much money?" inquires the trainee.

"Great question. What CAN you do?"

"Well, I could walk the neighbor's dog, mow some lawns, wash windows, clean out garages, pull weeds, babysit...," the boy continues his list as an enormous smile, the likes of which Oscar has never seen, appears on his mentor's face.

"You get it now, don't you?"

"I guess so," Oscar replies. "There are all kinds of ways to get my bike if I really think about it. All I needed was a goal, and then I could see it."

"Tell you what. You got an A on your last test, right? I'll reward your accomplishment with a ten-dollar bill," Roy says, reaching into his pocket once more. "You can take this money and buy candy, soda, whatever you wish. OR, you can take the money and put it down as a layaway payment on that bike you're sitting on. Then you can work for the rest of the money. The best part is I'll even show you how."

Oscar knows an offer he can't refuse when he sees one. He accepts the gift and goes to the cashier. Ever-so-pleased with himself, he places the cash on the counter, points to the bike he's chosen, and says, "I'd like to lay this one away, please."

As the two leave the store, the young man's face glows with joy.

"Here's what I want you to do," Roy instructs. "Make a flyer about all the things you can do to earn the money for your bike. I'll have it typed up real nice and have lots of copies made for you to leave around the neighborhood. We'll see what kind of response you get."

Oscar's flyer is far from glamorous, but what it lacks in beauty it makes up for in creativity.

The businessman gives Oscar's flyer to his assistant, Pam, asking her to improve the document on her computer.

"No way!" she tells him. "I'm leaving it just as is. It's precious and says everything it needs to say. In fact, it makes me want to hire him myself to gather up some wood in my yard. If this kid's willing to work for something, I'm willing to help him. In fact, I'm even going to put his flyers up all around town to get him even MORE jobs."

That reminds the businessman of the old adage, "God helps those who help themselves." This sparks him from within and sends him searching for one of his cards, which he hasn't seen in years.

Oscar returns home and goes to work.... "Hey, Oscar, you look overheated," Mrs. Torrans, a neighbor, says as she approaches him with a glass and a pitcher of ice water. "Why don't you take a break?"

Oscar stops the lawnmower and wipes the sweat from his forehead. "Thanks, Mrs. Torrans, I sure am thirsty," he says as he reaches for the glass she's filled and swallows it in a couple of big gulps. "But I can't rest for long. I've got two more yards to mow today, and then Mr. Miller wants me to help him clear out his attic."

"You're quite the little businessman," the kindly, older woman says. "When you get time, I'd also like you to mow my backyard too."

"Wow! Do you think there's a law against mowing at night?" Oscar asks, and he's not kidding.

"I think it would be hard to see the grass," his neighbor says, smiling. "But I'm in no hurry. I'll let you get back to work. Just leave the pitcher and glass on my porch if I'm not in when you get through."

"Thanks, Mrs. Torrans," Oscar says. "I'll be in touch."

The boy squared his shoulders confidently as he walked back to restart the lawnmower. Here he was just a kid, and a grownup had called him a businessman. Wow! The compliment got Oscar thinking. By the time he'd finished edging the lawn he was working on, the little businessman had hatched a plan.

Back at home.... "Oscar, don't eat so fast. You'll get an upset stomach," his mother tells him as he wolfs down his chicken casserole and salad.

"But I have things to do, Mom," he pleads. "I had a great idea while I was mowing today, and I want to go out and put my idea into action before it gets dark."

Two weeks later, while waiting for Oscar at the *Palace*, Roy nearly spills his coffee as he looks out the window. Totally amazed, he sees Oscar—riding a shiny new bike. "Oh my gosh!" Roy excitedly says to himself, as he watches Oscar pedaling like there's no tomorrow.

The boy races into the parking lot, jams on the brakes, jumps off the seat, and sets the lock. "I did it!" he announces as he runs into the *Palace*.

"You sure did, young man. And two months ahead of schedule," the businessman says warmly.

"It was just like you said, I set my mind on it and EVERYTHING fell into place. I got so many jobs on my street that it gave me a great idea. See what you think," the boy goes on breathlessly. "I kept getting more and more offers to cut the neighbors' yards and do other odd jobs. It was fantastic. One neighbor saw me working on somebody else's yard, and then he said he wanted his done that day! But I could only mow so much."

"That's what's known as a high-class problem," the man interrupts, chuckling.

"The way I figured it," Oscar continues excitedly, "I could either not take the job and lose the money, or come up with a plan to be able to take on more work."

"So, what did you do?" the advisor asks.

"That's the BEST part! All the other kids were jealous that I was making all this extra money and getting my bike now. They'd all have to wait 'til Christmas—if they were lucky, that is. I figured that if the neighbors each paid me $8 to do their yards, I'd hire the other kids and give each one $4 to do the work."

"Oh my," the businessman says, laughing. "Keep going."

"Okay. The way I see it, I got the work by coming up with the idea for the flyer. Well, actually YOU did, but THEY didn't know that," says the boy, with a grin. "So, I said if I was going to do all the hard work and GET the jobs for them, the least they could do was mow the simple lawns. They loved it, and so did the neighbors. Everybody started calling me 'bossman.' With this system, I made the money I needed in half the time, doing less work."

"That, my son, is what's referred to as working SMART. You're leveraging your efforts with others by having them duplicate what you do. Which reminds me, I found this in an old briefcase of mine," he continues, as he hands Oscar a tattered, dog-eared card. "It reminds me of this whole lesson, and I want you to have it."

As the boy reads the message, it all comes clear to him, summing up the experience he's just had.

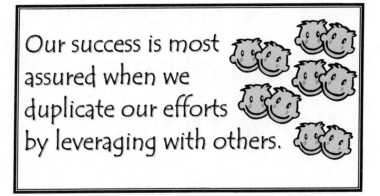

Our success is most assured when we duplicate our efforts by leveraging with others.

"Realize success by helping others achieve their goals."

—Greg S. Reid

Sales 101

Time flies by. As the boy grows more mature, the businessman becomes a father figure as well as a mentor. He vows to teach the young man everything he knows, every lesson he's ever learned. He believes that this bond, the connection between them, also helps to keep him energized and striving. For as the boy grows, so does the businessman.

"Hello, Roy," Oscar greets him, his voice now deeper.

"Hi, Oscar. Did you get the sale?"

"He told me to come back next week after he talked to the owner," the young man begins to explain.

"That would be NO then, wouldn't it?" Roy interjects abruptly.

Oscar had landed his first sales job, something he'd always wanted to do. He thought it would be easy to sell things to people because people seemed to like him. Little did he know.

"Well, actually, a sale WAS made," the advisor continues. "There's an old saying in the sales profession, 'A sale is made on every call. Either you sell the other person or he or she sells you.' This time, his *situation* was more believable than yours."

The student looks crushed. He glances away for a moment, bites his bottom lip, then leans in toward his friend, staring at him straight in the eye.

"Teach me."

The businessman grins. He knows exactly what Oscar is feeling at that moment—the exact moment in time when someone knows his or her life is about to change.

Excited for the young man, he shuffles through his billfold to find a card he's saved just for this occasion. As he presents it to Oscar, the businessman adopts a serious tone.

"Everything I have taught you so far will seem insignificant once we begin this journey," he says. "If you choose to accept the challenge before you, I'll guide you every step of the way. But once again, ONLY if you promise to share this lesson with someone else when it's time. Are you ready?"

"Teach me," Oscar says again earnestly.

Oscar looks down at the card and this time reads it out loud.

The difference between just TRYING to do something and actually DOING it is found in the OUTCOME.

The youthful mentee looks up, stroking his chin like a great philosopher.

"My coach once said that winners never talk about how hard they worked, but only how great it was to win. So, I guess if I start a statement off with, 'I tried...,' it really means, 'I failed,' because trying isn't really doing."

"You've got it, young man," Roy affirms. "It's important, though, that I give you an easy example to reinforce the idea." At that point, the mentor reaches down and pulls his shiny Mercedes keys from his suit coat pocket. He then says to Oscar, "Try to pick these keys up," endeavoring to contain his smile.

Oscar proceeds to take the keys from the older gentleman's hand. Roy exclaims, "You DID it! You didn't just 'try.' You see Oscar, you either do something or you don't. There's no such thing as try!"

"You know what? You're absolutely right, sir. And people use the word try all the time."

"Yes, just as that became clear to you, so will this," the older man responds. "*Sales* is a powerful word that frightens some people and excites others. To those who hate sales and salespeople, all I can say is, 'You hate what you fear and you fear what you hate.' Some people who hate sales probably just have the fear of BEING sold. Others, who think they could never be salespeople, may share the fear of rejection—the dread of being told NO."

Oscar just sits there mesmerized by the excitement on his counselor's face.

"It's good to understand the nature of sales even if it's just to be a more informed consumer, regardless of whether it strikes you as something you'd like to do yourself. Those who understand and can harness the power of sales, however, know that it is the highest paid occupation in the world. Sure, there are star athletes and movie moguls who make megabucks for what seems like easy work. But remember, someone had to 'sell' his or her skills to team owners and movie studios. In fact, no matter what we do in life, it's impossible to avoid sales. For example, remember when you bought that new bike?"

"I sure do!" Oscar answers.

"Well, someone had to sell it to you in the store, and someone else had to sell it to them. Before that, someone sold the parts to the manufacturer, someone sold the die-casting machine to the parts maker... the list goes on and on. You get the picture. Now the great thing is, sales is the one occupation that pays you for exactly what you've done."

"How's that?" the eager young learner asks, looking confused.

"Think about it. In sales, you get rewarded, or paid, for the sales you MAKE, not the ones you just attempt. You don't get paid for your effort, for *trying*, but only for producing—clear and simple."

"So wanting to learn sales is a good thing?"

"It's a great thing," his mentor replies enthusiastically. "But *closing* is even better. 'Sales' is synonymous with 'opportunity.' Every time you make a presentation, you have an opportunity to improve your income—by closing the sale! Every sale you close gives you the exhilaration of victory in conquering your fears and overcoming rejection."

Roy pauses and points his finger. "Look over there," he says. The young man turns his head, and Roy mysteriously pulls a new card out from behind Oscar's ear. "Closing a sale is magic," he whispers.

Oscar shoots him a look that says, "What do you think I am? Just a kid?"

The businessman chuckles. "Go ahead. Read it," he says.

Oscar reads it out loud.

It's as easy as
A.B.C.—
Always Be Closing

"I don't get it," Oscar tells him. "Aren't selling and closing the same?"

"The difference between the two is the size of the paychecks!" the businessman replies.

"You've seen salespeople on TV or at the mall, trying to show the value and sparkle of something they'd like you to buy. They use fancy lights, gadgetry, and a well-rehearsed presentation to show you all the reasons why you need the product—why you can't live without it.

You know the guy or gal at the local fair or carnival, with the slicer-dicer that cuts julienne fries? They stand up on a soapbox and yell at the passing crowd, 'Step right up. Check out the newest and greatest idea since sliced bread. Watch as I show you how it works.'

This form of sales is cute and when done correctly, it can even generate a sale every once in a while. But it is NOT the most effective approach to sales. I have found that the most successful salespeople aren't selling at all. They are *closing*."

The young man sits there with his mouth closed, and eyes and ears wide open.

"The most successful salespeople don't just plant the seed of suggestion, they motivate you to buy NOW. Finish your sundae, and I'll take you to a place where you can see how this works."

Oscar complies eagerly—always glad to have a chance to ride in Roy's fancy car. Roy makes a quick call on his cell phone, and then the pair drives a few miles to a high-end car dealership.

"The man who owns this place is a friend of mine," Roy tells Oscar. "He's agreed to let us observe his salespeople in action. We'll just browse around and eavesdrop on them as they close their sales."

"Cool!" Oscar enthuses.

Very soon, the youthful protégé and the businessman see a hesitant-looking fellow step onto the lot. A salesman approaches him.

"Hi, I'm Al. How are you doing today?" the salesman greets the customer, shaking his hand.

"Bryan," the customer says a little doubtfully. "I'm okay, but I'll feel much better when I finally have a new car."

"Great! What color were you thinking of? Any special options? Automatic or manual transmission? Convertible or hardtop?"

"Gee, I don't know," the buyer says. "Let me look around a while and think about it."

A few minutes later Al comes back to check on the buyer. "Find what you like?" he asks.

"Yeah, but there's so much to choose from. I think I'll go home and ask my wife what she thinks. After we have more of an idea of what we want, I'll bring her with me when I come back here tomorrow," Bryan tells him.

"Here's my card," Al says politely. "Be sure to ask for me. I'll be here from 9 to 5 tomorrow. I look forward to doing business with you." They shake hands and part ways.

Roy ushers Oscar to a quiet corner to discuss the transaction. "Was that good sales technique?" he asks the young person.

"I guess so..." Oscar begins hesitantly.

"Wrong!" Roy thunders. "Now let's go back out there and find a closer!"

Roy and Oscar see a well-dressed man staring longingly at a sporty red convertible in the showroom. "Great choice! This car is you!" a salesman booms out before the buyer says anything. "I'm George, by the way, good to see you!" he says confidently, shaking the customer's hand.

"I'm Ralph," says the man. "It's a great-looking car, but I was thinking that maybe a blue one would be more practical."

"I understand what you're saying," says George. "But from the way you were looking at the car, red seems to be the color you really want. How old are you, 30 or so? (Ralph nods, agreeing.) Great! You'll love having a red car; red gets all the attention. Just think of the looks you'll get cruising down the road in this beauty! You'll be the envy of the neighborhood."

"Yeah, but this has a stick shift," says Ralph, looking somewhat perplexed. "I was leaning more toward an automatic, again, because it seems like it would probably be more practical."

"Well, you could do that," George concedes dubiously, "but that would take the fun out of having this red one you really want. Besides which, it's more exciting driving with a stick shift. I'm sure you already know that."

"I agree," Ralph replies. "But my wife thought that maybe we should get a hardtop."

"Who's going to be driving the car? Probably you, most of the time, right?" George says, as he skillfully meets Ralph's objection.

"Well, I can't argue with that," Ralph says.

"Perfect!" George responds, as he heads for the close. "It sounds like you need to go with the convertible. That way you'll have the total package you wanted in the first place: a sharp, red, manual convertible! I must tell you, this is the one I'd drive too. We'd better get you into the office. After all, someone could come in tonight and buy your car. And it would probably take a couple of months before we could get in another one like this. But this one's all you, and you deserve to have it. Follow me, and we'll get the paperwork started. I'm sure you'll be happy with the car."

Roy turns to his pupil as Ralph and George head for George's office. "You see, Oscar, rule #1 to successful sales is, 'It's as easy as A.B.C.—Always Be Closing'—and never overwhelm the prospect with too many options."

"Now, as you can see," Roy continues, "this approach can be quite powerful. Just be sure to use it only to *help* people overcome their objections so they can get what they *really* want. Never use it to manipulate people into doing something against their will, or they'll never buy anything from you again. Use it to guide them into making a decision that will benefit them. In this case, the man had been staring longingly at the car he was attracted to. That was a good sign that he really wanted it—before any objections had a chance to clutter his mind."

"Wow, I get it," Oscar says brightly. "I need to *lead* people in the buying process. George led Ralph into buying the car by helping him overcome his objections, so Ralph could clearly make up his mind. But let me ask you, Roy, "Why do most people buy anything? I mean, what motivates them?"

"Great question," his advisor congratulates. "The reason people buy things, and the reason they do pretty much anything else, is this...." Once again, the businessman hands Oscar a card.

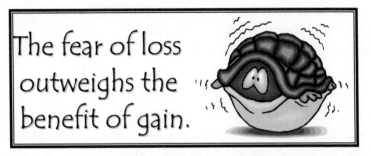

The fear of loss outweighs the benefit of gain.

"'Hurry now while supplies last.' 'Only two left at this price.' 'Don't delay; they're going fast.' 'Sale ends soon.' Ever heard any of these?" the businessman asks.

"Of course," Oscar says. "Lots of times."

"These are called 'trigger quotes.' They motivate you to take immediate action. Notice how they're all fear-based. For example, 'only two left' implies that if you don't drop everything and buy now, the items will be gone forever. It's quite simple, actually, if you think about it," the mentor explains. "Slogans like: 'Hurry Now or Miss Your Chance'; 'The Best Selection is Going Fast—Don't Miss Out'; 'Everything's Priced to Move This Weekend' carry more emotional impact than just saying, 'Come on down whenever you can; we're easy to find and have a huge selection to choose from.' See the difference? You need to give a sense of urgency."

"Yes, I totally see it," Oscar responds. "But how does the fear of loss affect why we do other things in life?"

"Everything in our society is based on this principle. 'Be a good, God-fearing Christian and love and help others' doesn't have the same emotional impact as, 'Be a good Christian or face eternal damnation,' now does it?"

The young man's jaw drops.

"It applies to all kinds of situations," Roy elaborates. "'Be a good driver and obey the laws' doesn't pack the same punch as, 'Slow down or you'll get a ticket, go to court, pay a fine, and have your insurance go up.'"

"So the fear of losing something, even if it's only a chance to make a purchase, outweighs the benefit of gaining something," Oscar summarizes.

"It sure does," the mentor agrees. "It's sad in a way, but once you understand this concept, you can begin to use it to YOUR benefit. When I wanted more sales from my staff, I used to offer a bonus. My people would work to attain the bonus a fair amount of the time. But if I said, 'Get three sales today, or I'm going to have to let you go,' they'd hit the target nine times out of ten. That's because fear of losing their jobs outweighed the benefit of simply making a few extra dollars. As you can see, there's a lot of POWER in this statement, so use it wisely."

"That's a good lesson," Oscar tells him, grinning from ear to ear. "What's another?'

"I'll tell you the next time we meet," Roy says. "You need to go home and think about what I've taught you today. You can apply these techniques at your job tomorrow."

"When you keep telling yourself you feel great, you eventually will feel just that—great!"

—Greg S. Reid

Don't Pitch Cats

"Okay, Roy," Oscar says eagerly after he's ordered his hot fudge sundae. "I've been thinking about that selling stuff you taught me at the car store. You said you'd have more to tell me this month."

"Oh, don't worry, I do," Roy tells the boy. "Read the message on this card out loud three times, then I'll explain."

Sell Situation→Situation Sells
Sell Emotion→Emotion Sells

When you have an
EMOTIONAL SITUATION,
you'll have yourself a SALE.

After repeating the message three times, Oscar waits for his lesson to begin.

"Situation and emotion are incredible sales tools when you put them together," Roy remarks. "One without the other doesn't have the same impact. I mean, think about it. A sales pitch or presentation with only a situation would be, 'Everything's got to go because....' One with strictly emotion would be when some crazy guy looks like a rat deserting a sinking ship, waving his arms and screaming at his customers. Either approach can annoy potential buyers and possibly even scare them away. But when you put situation and emotion together, you can create magic.

"Here's an example of an approach using both," he says as he points to an ad in the local paper on the table:

> After five years in business, we just received notice that our rent has doubled. So we have to say goodbye to all our friends and customers. This Thursday at 1 p.m., we are closing our doors forever. Everything must go. Our loss gives you an opportunity to pick up our merchandise for pennies on the dollar. It's our way of thanking you for all the years you've supported us.

"What an approach! It creates an emotional situation that can turn itself into lots of cash. After the sale, the store can reopen down the street at a lower rent. Then, they can have a 'Thanks to your generosity and support, we've saved the business' grand reopening sale. The bottom line, Oscar, is that people *want* a reason to buy—they actually need to be lead. Creating a situation gives them a reason to make a purchase in the first place. Placing emotion behind the situation gives them a reason to buy today."

"It's amazing how simple this whole thing is," Oscar notes. "I know it's not easy, but when you explain it, I see sales in a whole new light. Now I realize that a sales-person 'closed' me the other day when he persuaded me to buy five CDs. I only wanted one, but because there was a 10 percent discount for buying in volume, he actually helped me save money in the long-run."

"I think the same way," the mentor answers. "Every time I buy anything, I look to see if the salesperson is trying to 'sell' me something or 'close' me on the deal. By knowing the techniques, I'm in control to make the decision I want to make, rather than being controlled into making one."

"Roy, I find that sales prospects turn me down way more than I'd like. You must have some kind of a system to be so successful," Oscar says. "What are the steps to making a sale? How do I know what to look for, who to talk to—that sort of thing?"

The businessman replies, "I've tried everything, read every book, and listened to more tapes than you could count. I boiled everything I learned down to a five-step program that's always helped me out. I keep this card in my wallet all the time. Whenever I fall into a sales slump, I refer to it. By following these five steps and keeping it simple, I always pull myself out of it and get moving again."

The older man opens his fine leather wallet once more and pulls out a card, right from the front.

"Let me read this to you so you'll understand each point," Roy tells Oscar.

The Five Most Effective Steps to a Sale:

1. *Contact the decision maker.* That means don't waste time with nondecision makers, like you said you did when you first sat down today. You need to go directly to the person who signs the checks. Presenting to anyone else is like that slicer-dicer guy at the fair presenting his wares to the decision maker's cat. The kitty might really like what the man is doing, and be fascinated by the shiny objects, but it can't write him a check no matter how much it may want to. So don't pitch cats!

2. *Qualify and warm up.* Always greet people with a warm smile and positive words. When you know you're dealing with decision makers, check to make sure they're in a good mood and have time to speak with you. If they're crabby and in a hurry, they'll NEVER buy anything. Would you? By only speaking to happy, positive decision makers with time to hear you out, you greatly increase your chances of getting a deal, right?

The student nods enthusiastically. Roy continues...

3. *Pitch.* Make your sales pitch or presentation as brief and to the point as possible. This will give the buyer confidence that you know what you're talking about. Don't mince words—know what you're going to say before you say it.

4. *Close.* Assume the sale's been made even before it has. This gives buyers confidence that they're making a good decision. Expect them to say yes and more times than not, they will. Use closing lines like, 'What's your last name for my invoice?' or 'Now, is this going to be enough for you or could you use another one if I made the price ridiculous?' This is called *assuming the close.*

5. *Warm down.* Don't close the deal and just run off. Plant the seed for the next sale. Assure buyers that you appreciate their business. Let them know you are so confident of their decision that you'll be back to help them out again, when another *situation* arises. Keep in touch—after the sale—so you can build a relationship.

The most effective steps to a sale:

STEP 1→Contact the decisionmaker
STEP 2→Qualify and warm up
STEP 3→Present
STEP 4→Close
STEP 5→Warm down

"Okay. What you're saying is to talk only to happy, positive decision makers; give them an *emotional situation*; assume they believe it and have already bought; and assume you'll be back to make another sale later," Oscar paraphrases his teacher's thoughts.

"That's it!" the businessman enthusiastically responds. "Those are the five steps that keep me focused every time I go into a sales slump. It has nothing to do with what I'm selling. It has to do with ME presenting to the wrong person, trying to make grumpy people happy, or asking for a sale instead of EXPECTING one. What it comes down to, Oscar, is seeking out people who fit YOUR profile, not trying to make buyers out of nonbuyers. *Don't pitch cats!* Remember what happens when we try?"

"Try means fail," Oscar says, then thinks for a moment. "But there's no way I can turn *every* presentation into a sale. How do I overcome all the nos? Back when I was in school, my friend with the bike-spoke idea, Marcos, just gave up after the first kid turned him down. I don't want to give up. How do I keep going?"

"Great question; one of your best yet! And it's got a two-part answer. First, let's talk about how to overcome a buyer's objections, the reasons he or she cannot buy," Roy says.

"Every time someone states a reason for not buying, AGREE. Say, 'I know that,' but never, <u>ever</u> repeat the objection because that will only reinforce it. It's almost impossible to overcome a reinforced negative. Here's a scenario," the businessman offers:

> Let's imagine a clerk at the local camera shop, who wants to move the camera a buyer's looking at. "Take that camera home with you, and I'll throw in a roll of film for free," the salesperson says.
>
> "I wish I could, but I wasn't planning to spend so much money. My taxes are due," the buyer responds.
>
> The salesperson then says, "I know what you mean. Tell you what. I'll go ahead and throw in two rolls of film and even process them for 10 percent off. I just need to move this last item. You get a great deal, and I can make room on the counter for the new models that are due in. Would you like me to gift-wrap it?"

"Easy, huh? That's a nondefensive way to overcome the objection and assume the close without being aggressive. What has the salesperson created?"

"An emotional situation," Oscar answers.

"Exactly. Now let me tell you the wrong way the clerk could have reacted to the same objection: 'Taxes, huh? I hear about that a lot this time of year. What if I threw in two rolls of film and free developing? Do you think you could swing it then?' Oscar, what has the salesperson done wrong?"

Oscar thinks a minute, then answers, "He reinforced the buyer's negative, and asked for the sale instead of assuming the close."

"Very good," Roy says happily. "The normal response from the buyer would be, 'I'd like to, but you know how it is. Maybe I'll come back in a couple of weeks when I have more cash. Thanks for understanding.' See the difference? When you look at sales objectively, you'll be able to see when it's time to close the deal."

Oscar smiles slowly, a look of comprehension on his face.

"As far as overcoming discouragement due to lack of sales, I don't have a card on that."

"I don't believe it!" Oscar teases.

"But I do have a technique," Roy responds, "and I've shared it with every salesperson I have ever trained. It's so ingrained in my mind I don't need to see it written down, but I'll write it down for you nonetheless." His mentor takes a beautiful, shiny pen from his top pocket and starts scribbling on a napkin.

> # You CAN do it.
> # You WILL do it.
> # Just Shuck Another Oyster!

"It works like this: Imagine a basket full of oysters in front of you," the businessman instructs. "Each oyster represents a sales call. Every time you make a presentation, it's like you're shucking one of the oysters. When you open one up and there's no pearl inside, do you give up and walk away from the basket of unopened oysters? Of course you don't. You pick up another oyster and do it again! There have to be pearls inside some of them, right?"

"Right," Oscar agrees.

"Well, the same goes for sales calls. Just because you don't close one deal, doesn't mean you don't go on to the next. In truth, a *no sale* or *no pearl* is a good thing!"

"Why?" the younger man asks.

"It means you're one step closer to finding a pearl! *No sale* could be best viewed as inspirational, because it means you're getting the negatives out of the way and paving your way to the next success. That, my friend, is the simplest way I can explain how to overcome discouragement," the mentor concludes. "You CAN do it. You WILL do it. Just shuck another oyster!"

"Makes sense," the student remarks. "The best way to overcome negatives is to keep going. Kind of like the card you gave me a while back, but this time it would say, 'The two times to make another sales call are 1) when you want to and 2) when you don't.'"

The businessman lets out a great big laugh and says, "You've got it!"

"Good. But I have another question," Oscar says with a smile. "Once I close the sale, what's the best way to KEEP the customer happy enough that I can make another sale?"

"I knew you were going to ask me that," the businessman says with a twinkle in his eye. "You'll be relieved to know I've got a card for this."

"Good. I was getting worried," Oscar jokes, reaching out for the card.

Tell them what they NEED to hear, not what they WANT to hear.

"Another way to put that is: underpromise, overdeliver," Roy says. "It sounds easy, yet so few grasp the power this statement holds. Again, let me give you an example:

Suppose you were in my business of selling advertising promotional items, and you wanted to move your excess ballpoint pen inventory. Here's a way you could use an *emotional situation* closing technique that also incorporates the principle of underpromise, overdeliver.

You say, "Hey, Bob, this is Oscar, with XYZ Company. I'm glad I caught you. I just received my shipment of holiday stock, and I need to make room for it. Take a box of my extra pens. I'll do the printing and setup for a fraction of the cost for helping me out. Take them for next to nothing!"

Bob says, "Are they GREAT pens?"

You say, "Not really. They're leftovers. That's why I'm doing them so inexpensively. I will tell you this though. They're *pens*, they *write*, and I'll print your name on them for *free*. No matter what pens I send you, they probably won't change the way you live. People are just going to walk off with them, right? I mean, if people are going to take them anyway, you may as well have your name on them."

"That's the situation," Roy explains. "Then when the customer receives his order and the pens are actually halfway decent, and the company's name is big and bold on the side, Bob says to himself, 'Hey, these things are pretty good.' He feels as though he got a bargain. That's the emotion. The next time you call to sell Bob something else, what are the odds that he's going to trust you?"

"Pretty good," Oscar answers.

"You get the idea. So many other people would spend time focusing on selling the pens. They could lose the customer, or at least the reorder, by overpromising and underdelivering. In the zeal to make a sale, the person says things like, 'They're great! You'll love them. They'll change the way you do business. You can't go wrong.' Then, when the customer finds out they're *just pens*, it's disappointing. By underpromising and overdelivering, you create customer confidence and increase the odds of making another sale in the future. It's a win-win situation, and *that's* what it's all about!"

Estelle, the server, comes over to check on the two. "How are you boys doing?" she asks.

"ALWAYS good," Roy answers brightly, as Estelle walks away with a smile on her face.

"Why do you always say that?" Oscar asks. "Most people say 'fine' or something."

"Ask someone, 'How are you doing?' and listen to the response. Most of the time the person will say something like, 'Not bad,' 'Fair to middlin,' 'Can't complain,' or 'Fine.' Most of those responses are negative, and 'fine' is so overused, it's become meaningless.

"After noticing this for years," Roy continues, "I decided to come up with a truly positive response to the question, 'How are you doing?' I say, 'Always good.' You wouldn't believe the looks I get. It still bewilders me. When I'm at the grocery store and the clerk asks me how I am, I say 'always good.' The clerk usually looks up and says, 'Really?' I've even had people in line turn to me skeptically and ask, 'How can anyone be good all the time?' I answer with my favorite quote by Abraham Lincoln, 'People are about as happy as they make up their minds to be.'

"I choose to maintain a constant positive outlook. It's amazing the way our minds work. When you keep telling yourself you feel great, you actually will feel great! What a concept!"

The boy rewards his mentor with an appreciative smile. "You're teaching me so much," the mentee tells him. "I don't want to take too much of your time, but could you help me set some sales goals and make a plan of action to meet them?"

"Of course," the gentleman beams. When that task is finished, he picks up the tab and rises to leave.

Oscar reaches for a pen, quickly scribbles some words on a napkin, folds it in half and hands it to Roy. He then shakes his hand firmly.

"Thank you for your inspiration," Oscar says with a glimmer in his eye. "Since 'always good,' is your saying, this one will be mine."

The businessman steps into his car, a lump of emotion forming in his throat as he unfolds the napkin and reads what Oscar has written.

"The best leaders begin their quests by being the best followers."

—Greg S. Reid

Leadership

Although he's now a full-fledged grown-up and a married man, Oscar's expression is one of boyish excitement as he walks through the door of the *Palace of Frozen Delights* for his monthly meeting with his mentor. The businessman can tell that Oscar has something big to share.

"Sit down and let's hear it," Roy mock-commands.

"Great news! They made me manager of the sales department!"

"Terrific! All those years of being the top producer paid off in more than just commissions."

"I guess so," Oscar replies, smiling. "They want me to manage our downtown location which has over fifty salespeople. I'm so excited at the opportunity, but I'm also quite nervous. I don't have any management experience."

"This is a big day, indeed," says the businessman. "A cause for celebration. Today's ice cream is on me."

"Along with some of your words of wisdom, I hope. Since I got married last year, and we now have a child on the way, I want to thank you in advance for seeing me through this transition. I'm sure that, with your guidance and unconditional support, we will tackle this challenge with nothing but success. So, thank you," Oscar says, reaching out to shake his mentor's hand.

"Hmm, an emotional situation/assumptive close. You just may be ready for the next level," Roy says, grinning. Then he offers the younger man another of his "famous" cards.

To get what YOU want, you FIRST need to help others get what THEY want!

"Yep! This sums up what you've been teaching me over the years," Oscar says. "But tell me, what's a realistic way of helping others set and reach goals?"

"This is my favorite topic, Oscar. We each have individual goals and desires. What's important to you and me may not be important to someone else. But one common denominator is that you need to provide the best opportunities for your people to achieve their goals. And more than manage, you need to lead them. Set the pace and show them how it's done. Ask what their dreams are and offer to help accomplish them. This can help them get motivated—so they'll want to perform.

Teach your people to write down their goals. It'll give them a tangible reminder of the target they're aiming to hit," Roy says, then pauses for a sip of coffee, and hands Oscar another card.

A DREAM written down with a date becomes a GOAL. A goal broken down becomes a PLAN. A plan backed by ACTION makes your dream come true.

"Think of someone with a bow and arrow shooting into thin air, saying, 'Great shot! Look at me, Boy, I'm doing great!'" Roy continues. "Compare that person with someone who puts up a bull's-eye target in front of him and keeps focused on the goal until he hits the center. How can anyone know how well he or she is doing without having a target to shoot at?"

"Right," Oscar agrees, "but how does that work in business?"

"I thought you'd never ask!" the mentor laughs, teasing his earnest student. "The same principle applies in business. Help them write down clear and concise goals to give themselves a target to hit. When they know what their goals are, and that they'll be held accountable for reaching them, you're leading them toward success. I find it's harder to give up— and easier to stay focused on a goal—when someone keeps asking me how I'm coming along with it. You'll find, too, that other employees will pitch in to help individuals achieve their goals. People love to help each other out in a team-spirit-sort-of way."

"Okay, Roy, but suppose I set goals that are too high for what my people want to accomplish?"

"Good question! Keep in mind that the goals you help your people set need to be challenging but not unobtainable. You wouldn't give the new guy the hardest area and the highest quota. You'd help him set a goal that is less challenging at first, and then let him stretch and grow as he works his way up. Always encourage people to keep striving for the next level!"

"That makes a lot of sense," Oscar observes. "I remember when I first took on the sales job, and I sat here with you as we charted out my goals. Then, every month, I knew I'd better hit that goal, because you had shared it with me. It wasn't just my goal, it was *OUR* goal. After a while, I didn't even focus on the commissions anymore. I just wanted to be able to tell you, every time we met, that I'd done better."

"You see, Oscar, it all comes down to one thing— accountability. To be a good manager, and an even better leader, you must give that word paramount importance. Pay careful attention to these words," as Roy hands Oscar another card.

> The true measure of a person's integrity is the extent to which he or she is accountable.

He continues, "Here's the way I lead my people:

- ✓ When things go right, it's to THEIR credit.
- ✓ When things go wrong, it's MY fault.
- ✓ When things go along without a care, it's to ALL OUR CREDIT together."

"I like that," Oscar chimes in. "So, the whole idea is don't take credit for all the good things that happen, but do take responsibility for the mishaps. That way you stay humble, and people will want to give you their best. They'll feel appreciated AND do all they can to support you. They know for sure that you won't let them down when the going gets tough."

"Exactly. That's how to be a good leader. Good managers are pretty easy to find if you look hard enough. But what you have, Oscar, are the makings of a great LEADER."

"I don't understand," Oscar protests. "Aren't managers and leaders the same?"

"Not by a long shot. The difference is even more dramatic than the difference between a salesperson and a closer. You see...

Many people mistake management for leadership," he tells his protégé. "They are two completely different things. Think about a pro sports team. The coach directs the team on the field, motivating the players to perform as a single unit, keeping them focused on the goal. The team owner, or the leader, so to speak, is the one who creates the original goal in the first place. He or she envisions the end result or TARGET, if you will. That person then brings in others to assist in reaching the goal, and empowers them to achieve the desired outcome.

"You see, Oscar," Roy continues, motioning to Estelle for more coffee, "a true leader doesn't have to do everything. However, a leader must know how to clearly and concisely explain what needs to be done, and then empower others to fulfill the objectives. The leader doesn't need to do all the work. However, he or she does need to monitor progress based on jointly defined goals—or targets—given to those under his guidance.

"A sports MANAGER simply carries out the vision presented to him or her, such as to win the division championship. Then that individual has the responsibility to make that goal a reality. This is accomplished by hiring various players, planning strategies according to the dynamics of the opposing team, controlling player assignments, and supervising and evaluating player performance. You know, managing."

"Okay," Oscar says, pondering, "I think I get it. But leaders and managers also need to work together, right?"

"Exactly! A leader without a great manager doesn't have the same impact. A leader could just be some crazy dreamer with loads of money and great ideas, but have no one to follow up and take action to make those dreams come true. You need people to do the legwork too. So, to maximize success, you need both leaders and those who are striving to be leaders," Roy comments.

"It works the other way too," he continues. "A great manager without specific objectives—that is, a manager who lacks great leadership—can become stagnant and regimented. He or she could wind up bored, performing the same operations over and over because no direction was given. The manager has no target, so to speak."

"I see what you're saying. But Roy, surely people aren't just born leaders. How do you become one?" Oscar asks.

"As I told you before, Oscar, it takes certain traits—traits I see in you—for great leadership. The best leaders begin their quests by being the best followers.

"Imagine a great military general starting out as a private: listening, learning, following orders, and moving up in the ranks. A true leader needs to be able to listen to others. That person also needs to be able to paint a vivid and realistic picture of his or her vision for the future. Easier said than done, I know. That's why there are so few great leaders.

"You know, a good, very successful friend of mine, Dr. Peter C., shared a simple chart with me to show the difference between leadership and management. I think I've got a copy of it in here." Roy opens his briefcase, pulls out a sheet of paper and hands it to Oscar.

MANAGEMENT	⇨	LEADERSHIP
Sees Things as They Are	⇨	Sees Things as They Could Be
One-Way Communication	⇨	Two-Way Communication
Process Development	⇨	People Development
"Do the Thing Right"	⇨	"Do the Right Thing"
Stagnation	⇨	Renewal, Growth
A Regimen	⇨	A Relationship
Directional	⇨	Free, Creative
Paradigm	⇨	Paradigm Shift
Limited View	⇨	Big Picture
Efficiency	⇨	Effectiveness
Subordinate	⇨	Follower
Factual	⇨	Conceptual
Reality	⇨	Possibilities
Delegate	⇨	Empower
Condition	⇨	Develop
Structure	⇨	Flexible
Acceptance	⇨	Trust
Stability	⇨	Transitional Chaos

"Let's see if I've got this right," Oscar ventures after he looks at the chart.

"Leaders see the big picture, they're able to communicate that vision to others, and it seems like they have a special ability to spur others on to success."

"Yes!" his mentor beams. "I'm very pleased about the fine way you've honed in on the basics of leadership."

"It's easy with such a great teacher like you," Oscar replies. "I understand what leaders need to do, but what EXACTLY are the personality traits needed to become a leader? What traits do you think I have?"

"Son, I know you have them," Roy encourages his pupil. "Leaders can come from any background and any country. They can rise to a position of leadership in any organization. All leaders have these five traits in common:

1. Positive attitude.
2. Genuine concern for everyone's success.
3. Consistency.
4. Ability to clearly define goals.
5. Ability to empower others to meet defined goals.

"When people have these five traits, there's no limit to what they can do, whether they're well-intentioned or not. Charles Manson and Hitler were leaders who convinced people to do unspeakable things. Positive examples, however, include Abraham Lincoln, Teddy Roosevelt, Mother Teresa, Margaret Thatcher, and the owners of last season's victorious sports teams, just to name a few.

"Oscar, I want you to use your talent to lead others in a positive manner. Positive results will follow. My dad once said, 'If you want others to follow in your footsteps, don't step in poop,'" the businessman says with a grin.

"Here's another little tidbit you need to know." Once again, he hands Oscar a card.

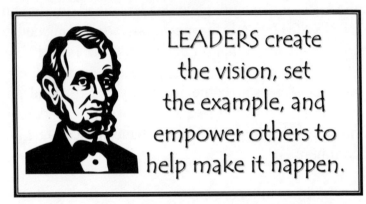

LEADERS create the vision, set the example, and empower others to help make it happen.

"I worked at a huge corporation when I was younger," the advisor relates. "Once in a while, the department heads would come into the warehouse where I was working and tour the plant. They'd nod at a few people as they passed, then walk out the other end. People would get all fired up from the adrenaline of the 'suits' walking through and nodding at them."

"Gosh, that doesn't seem like much," Oscar remarks.

"I know, but that little bit of recognition was enough to increase workers' productivity. This company had another ritual they performed every six months: a 'state of the corporation' address. All the department heads would gather in the conference room. The president of the corporation—our leader—would then come in. He shared with us how the company was doing, celebrate a few departments' successes, and paint a picture in our heads about where the company was and where he saw it going. He created the target for us to hit! Then he'd ask for our help in attaining his vision. Before he left, he handed each department head a copy of the company's goals and recognized us individually for supporting the company's vision.

"Wow! What an impact that had on me!" Roy exclaimed. We'd always be so excited after these meetings that we'd go back to our work stations and really go to town. The enthusiasm usually lasted for a couple of months, or until the department heads lost sight of the target.

"I'd always say to myself, 'When I run a company, I'm going to have a state-of-the-company meeting EVERY month—to keep my people constantly fired up. I'll reward them for hitting the bull's-eye every time they do!

"To this day," the businessman continues, "I find that when you share information with others, they share information with you. Like I said before, people love goals. Keeping them updated on the progress toward a goal gives them a sense of purpose, and the feeling that they're an important part of the end result.

"Regular updates help the leader too. That person will be able to see if his or her other visions are obtainable, and if others are going to follow him or her in the quest. You will have people standing behind you, because they'll feel as though they are part of something important!" Roy hands Oscar another card.

Oscar looks enlightened. "That's amazing!" he enthuses. "Just by sharing ideas and information, the respect you are showing people by including them in the loop will get people to back your play. They will feel involved, part of the BIG picture, and not just a faceless employee or associate."

"That's how it works," Roy answers. "Just look at history. During times of prosperity, everyone shares in the success. During a crisis, people tend to pull together toward a common purpose. There's an old saying, 'People will do more for a cause than for money.'"

"Well, I hate to disagree with you, Roy," Oscar begins. But his mentor interrupts, asking, "Would you let me shoot you in the chest for $10,000?"

"Nooooo," Oscar says, staring wide-eyed at Roy.

"Would you throw yourself in front of a bullet if someone came in here and aimed it at that child in the corner?" Roy demands, pointing at a towheaded kid sitting at a table, licking butterscotch syrup off the side of his ice-cream dish. "Especially if he was your son?"

"Of course I would!"

"There you go," Roy says, smiling and spreading his hands in a ta-da gesture. "It's an extreme example, but it proves that people will do more for a cause than for money."

Oscar shoots Roy the "Okay, you-got-me" look his mentor had gotten used to over the years. "But how can I use that knowledge in leading others?" he asks after a moment.

"Simple. Maintaining goals is a management job. Creating a vision, or CAUSE, is the leader's responsibility. Of course, if you have your own small business, you get to do both!" Roy spoons up a bite of his banana split and looks at Oscar expectantly.

"Okay, wait a second," Oscar exclaims, sitting up in his chair. "I think I'm getting it. If I go into this position with a leadership mentality, goal setting will be the least of my concerns.

By creating a vision for my office, I'll rally everyone to the cause of becoming the most productive, efficient, and professional sales group in the entire corporation. I'll fire them up about setting new records, becoming THE office for the others to emulate."

"Great!" his mentor encourages. "How will this affect your sales staff?"

"Everyone in the office will feel the excitement of growth. Setting a vision will weed out the self-interested people who worry only about their own success, and show who the real team players are. People will begin setting their own goals in order to fulfill the overall goal or cause of the unit: to become the BEST!"

"You know Oscar, it's great to see your expression when these things come together for you," the businessman says. "But there is a warning that comes with this message as well."

"What's that?" Oscar asks, concerned.

"You must, repeat MUST, keep your composure through the inevitable transitions when things go wrong. It's not a question of if something will go wrong, only when. We're all dealt obstacles in life; that's part of life itself. It's how we handle those obstacles that exposes our true character." Roy hands Oscar another card.

The true measure of all great leaders is how well they weather the storms.

"Remember, Oscar, as Earl Nightingale said, 'We become our most dominant thoughts,'" the esteemed teacher advises. "When we see ourselves as bright, successful, and confident, we become just that. And, of course, the opposite applies as well. For example, we once experienced a major breakdown at the company I used to work for as a sales manager. Someone older and wiser told me, 'You're the captain of the ship. Never let the others see fear in your eyes, or they'll jump ship out of panic.' And that's very true. It's a lesson that's stayed with me ever since."

"Hmm," Oscar murmurs, nodding in agreement.

"Think about a slowly sinking ship, leaks popping up out of nowhere, with the captain running around frantically, in a panic. When subordinates see their leader lose composure, trust me, they will too! It's easy to do the right thing and stay positive, upbeat, and focused when everything's going your way. But when the chips are down, you see a person's true character. Here's one of the greatest quotes of all time," Roy concludes, handing Oscar another card.

We learn more about
the character of people on
one OFF day,
than on all their
ON days put together.

"I've found that even on a rough day, when we act positive, in spite of feeling unraveled inside, it helps. It helps us deal with the situation at hand with the best attitude we can muster. It's the old 'fake it till you make it' mentality," Roy comments.

"Yes. It's like your saying, 'Always good,'" Oscar replies.

"Exactly," Roy answers. "When we keep telling ourselves and everyone else how great we're doing, even when we're not, sooner rather than later we become 'Always good'!"

"I hear what you're saying, Roy, I really do. But what can I do when people tell me these great visions will never work? What about the people who say, 'But we're used to doing it this way. Why rock the boat'?" Oscar queries.

"Let me tell you something, son," the gentleman begins, "there is nothing as expensive as negativity." Here is my advice to you: It's something I heard many years ago, I don't remember who said it, but it stuck with me all the same." He slips his student another card.

Avoid people
who have negative
attitudes.

"Avoid people who have negative attitudes. They just drag you down," Roy explains. "Now, I'm not referring to people with positive criticism, or people who play devil's advocate. I mean people who seem happiest when others suffer—people who rarely have anything good to say. You know the difference."

"Sure I do," Oscar agrees.

"When I began my career in specialty sales, I remember telling my friends and family, 'I'm going to make $1,000 a week selling pens,'" Roy relates. "They all laughed at me and told me to get a *real* job. They told me I'd never make it. Ever hear that one?"

"Of course. Who hasn't?" Oscar answers with a grin.

"But I did then what I still do with my new ideas today. I just kept telling different people my plan until I came across someone who said, 'Good for you!' and gave me some ideas on how to make it happen. She told me some of the dos and don'ts of the industry. You know, 'positive' criticism. What a difference! Let me tell you, right then and there I realized that whenever I wanted to get ahead with any of my ideas, I needed to seek out people who shared my enthusiasm, or at least those who could offer valuable perspectives or guidance on the opportunity."

"It's that 'shucking oysters' thing again, isn't it?" Oscar ventures.

"Yes. When I say, 'Hey I'm thinking of doing... (whatever), and the response is, 'Don't bother. You'll never make it,' I think to myself, 'Oh, well, one oyster gone. No pearl—or pearl of wisdom.' So I move on to the next, then the next, then the next, until I find what I'm looking for. By the way, pretty soon my family started introducing me to their friends as their son, the pen man, their great little success story!"

"With your help, I hope to be as successful as you one day, Roy," Oscar tells his friend.

"You will be, my son, I can just feel it," the mentor says. "Just never let another person tell you your limitations. With a positive attitude, there is nothing we can't do. Even when we fall short, we will still feel successful for having gone beyond expectations.

"Was Oprah Winfrey supposed to be one of the wealthiest women of all time? Was Bill Gates supposed to create an empire that would change all of our lives forever? What if Jonas Salk had decided to give up that crazy polio vaccine idea? Just think how different this world would be if everyone listened to the naysayers and doom-and-gloomers.

"Follow your heart. Follow your dreams. Only you know what you want to accomplish," Roy says, then recites the message on the card he hands his pupil.

There is nothing as POWERFUL as a POSITIVE ATTITUDE.

"Thanks, Roy," Oscar says, glancing at his new watch with a look on his face that says there's somewhere else he needs to be.

"One more thing," his advisor whispers, grabbing Oscar's arm and covering the Rolex™ his dedicated student received with his promotion. "This is very important, and yet so few do it." Roy scribbles two words on the bottom of the restaurant check.

GIVE BACK

"Oscar, if I give you a $20 bill, would you give me a $5 bill in return? In other words, would you be willing to give some of your gain away?"

"Sure!" Oscar responds.

"That's good! I'd say you are a generous person. That's a sign of a winner," Roy smiles. "It looks like you're in a bit of a hurry, so I'll make this quick. But it's important."

"All your advice is important. I'll be glad to hear you out," Oscar tells the businessman.

Roy smiles at his young friend and launches into the next lesson. "As we've discussed, a leader's responsibility is to help everyone who follows him or her feel as if that person has a vested interest in whatever cause the leader creates.

"At my company, we created a mission to increase our customer base and thereby increase our revenue. We gave ourselves a target. I implemented a program called the Green Club. To get into the Green Club, a salesperson needs to reach a rolling seven-week sales volume average of $5,000 and generate ten new customers. When they reach this level, the company rewards them by making one of their car payments. We give back.

"We keep the averages and statistics posted all the time so the staff can tell what volume and how many customers they need to close each week to keep their average the same or, hopefully, to increase it. A rolling average is an example of the 'baby steps' theory. All the salespeople need to do is a little better than they did seven weeks ago, and their average goes up. Best of all, they NEVER lose sight of that bull's-eye!

"Before we implemented this program, my staff averaged $3,500 to $4,000 each week, and about three new clients. Why? Because it was the average they'd set earlier for themselves as an obtainable goal. There were no incentives to increase it. They were making a good living, so why stretch themselves?"

"You mean, they were comfortable in just getting by?" Oscar asks.

"Yes, they needed to be reminded that we all could do better. After only four weeks of putting the mission or TARGET before them and starting the incentive program, half the sales staff reached the new average. We gladly made their car payments and publicly celebrated their accomplishments. Recognizing their achievements inspired them to continue their successes. The 'fear-of-loss' mentality comes into play, as well. No one wants to lose the car-payment bonus or risk falling out of the club.

"Another benefit of the plan was that the salespeople all enjoyed watching the company grow," Roy adds. "The thing just kept snowballing. As our client base expanded, the new customers brought in more revenue. Since the employees shared in the new revenue, they wanted to bring in even more customers, and with those new customers came more revenue. You get the picture?"

"Right. And because your staff was generating so much new business, it was no hardship making the car payments as a reward!" Oscar says with a self-satisfied smile.

"Very good," Roy beams at him. "Making the car payments cost us NOTHING! We made money and doubled our client portfolio in one year. You see, the salespeople were averaging $3,500 to $4,000 a week in volume. To get the car payment, they had to hit $5,000, right? They produced the extra sales volume and brought in more profit for the company. In turn, we shared the wealth, using a portion of the profit for the car payments. The staff was ecstatic and so were we! Company revenues increased and net profits rose by 15 percent of the increased volume, even after we made their payments. When you also consider that we generated so many new clients at the same time, this was the epitome of a 'win-win' relationship."

"That's terrific," Oscar tells Roy. "But what happens when people get stuck at the new level?"

"Son, you're really learning," Roy enthuses. "The NEW target program at the company is called the President's Club. To get into that club, a salesperson needs to reach a rolling seven-week sales volume of $8,000 and generate ten new customers a week. When that person does, I pay his or her rent, not to exceed $800, for a month, and we throw in the car payment on top of that! And what do you think this costs us?"

"Nothing!" Oscar exclaims.

"You've got it. When you can give people a chance to better their lives, and encourage them until they do it, you'll enjoy going to work every day. You'll want to see how they're doing, plus you'll know that you're attaining your own dreams at the same time. So, Oscar, to wind this up: Be a great leader. Give credit where credit is due, and always GIVE BACK. Share the wealth. Be creative. Make each employee or associate feel as though he or she makes a difference. And remember... to get what we want, we first need to help others get what they want."

Thinking about the lessons he had learned, we find Oscar sitting in his office, sipping coffee, going over sales figures, while listening to soft jazz in the background. Suddenly, he hears an ear-splitting shriek from down the hall. "Oscar! File room! Now!" his boss, Mr. Lexmark, howls.

Oscar jumps up, spilling coffee all over the report on his desk and onto his lap. He races down the hall in a hurried hopping motion, his thighs "ablaze" from the hot liquid. He peers in the door of the file room and sees Mr. Lexmark, now ominously quiet, with a look of disappointment, shaking his head in front of a file cabinet.

"What's the problem, sir?" Oscar asks meekly.

"Oscar," Lexmark barks, turning to face his frightened employee, "will you tell me why, on God's green Earth, nobody can ever find a file around here? Every department has a different system, a different story. Just once I'd like to find the file I'm looking for when I need it!"

"I'm on it, sir," Oscar tells him as his boss starts off down the hall, mumbling to himself.

Oscar walks like a zombie back to his office. He has no idea how to fix the filing problem. He sits at his desk, pondering, and then suddenly a light bulb goes on in his head. He rummages through his briefcase until he finds a card Roy had given him years earlier.

He knows the answer he had been seeking is right before him.

Oscar rushes off to Human Resources and tells the department head he's looking for someone to head up a special assignment—cleaning up the filing system. After she stops laughing, Mary Gale boots up current employees' job applications. While Oscar looks on, she institutes a keyword search for organizational skills, and narrows the database down to the three people best qualified for the project.

Oscar interviews all three, behaving as if they're up for the best opportunity of their lives, never letting on the true nature of the project. Choosing Mary B. to help him with his goal quest, he calls her into his office.

"Mary, I've got an important project I want you to help me with," he begins.

"Yes, you mentioned that in the interview," she says warily. "But you never did say exactly what I'd be doing."

"This!" Oscar says, smiling as he points to one of his favorite cards, which he had enlarged and framed to hang on his wall.

What is important is how well we perform a task, not how big it is.

Mary stares at Oscar with the same familiar look of confusion he is used to from his co-workers.

"You see," he says, "I need you to do a job that most people would consider beneath them. Since you're the most qualified person for the job, I'm asking you to teach me, and for that matter, the whole company, something of vital importance. We really need your expertise on this project. Will you help?"

"Sure," she replies, "but what will I be doing?"

"Let's tell everyone at once," Oscar replies, and ushers her to the general open work area.

"Everyone, attention please!" Oscar hollers. As the shuffling and phone calls subside, he continues.

"I have great news," he says. "Today I've been challenged! But the best news is that Mary, here, has volunteered to help me meet that challenge. In return, I'd like all of us to help her. Can I count on you?" he chants like a cheerleader.

"Yes!" his loyal staff answers.

"Great! Here's what she's going to do," Oscar tells them, turning to Mary, who stands expectantly in front of her peers. "Fix the filing system!"

Snickers and whispers fill the air as Mary pales and looks at Oscar as if to say, "You've got to be kidding!"

"Really listen everybody," Oscar continues. "How many of you have not been able to find a file folder you're looking for?" Hands go up all over the room. "Even if you put it back correctly, it's not there the next time you look for it, right?"

More laughter and murmurs of agreement.

"Exactly. We've all had that unpleasant experience. Mary here is going to change that for us."

"I am?" She says as the crowd breaks up in laughter.

"Sure," Oscar tells her. "You have the strongest organizational background of anyone here. I've done my research, that's why I know YOU can correct the filing problem. The best part is we're all going to help you. So let me ask you...What can we all do first?"

Mary ponders for a moment, and then asks, "What's easier for everyone? Alphabetical or numeric?" The crowd goes for alphabetical arrangement with the files labeled by last names.

"Okay," Mary says enthusiastically. "Everyone, please have all files to me by Friday at 10 a.m. That way I can do this all at once. Any volunteers to help?" Several hands go up.

"Wow! I only need one," she says, and chooses her new assistant.

"Great," Oscar closes. "Let's be sure to turn all our files in by Friday morning so these two can tackle a job most people would run from." The crowd applauds and shouts words of encouragement.

"Mary, I really trust you. You fix this system any way you want to. You are the best person for the job," Oscar tells her as the workers file back to their stations.

"And you know what?" Oscar asks Roy as he fills him in on the story. "She and her assistant, Tom, took every file out of every cabinet on the entire floor and refiled them in the new system they'd invented. They even came up with a "check-in/check-out" program to keep track of files on a continuing basis. It worked out great. My staff was pleased, and you should have seen the look on Mary's and Tom's faces when I gave them tickets to a sold-out concert that weekend for a job well done."

"Sounds like a big success," Roy ventures.

"Well, it was for me!" Oscar crows excitedly. "But I haven't even gotten to the best part. Lexmark was so impressed with the filing system 'he had inspired' that he asked every department of the corporation to implement it—and had Mary oversee the project! I hope she gets a promotion out of this. Who'd have thought? All this came from the simplest of tasks. But like the card says, 'What is important is how well we perform a task, not how big it is.'"

Roy smiles.

"You can fulfill your potential by focusing on and following your dream. That's where your purpose lies."

—Greg S. Reid

Purpose and Direction

"I think it's time for a vacation," Oscar says with a grin as he plunks himself down in his usual spot at the *Palace*.

"Why do you say that?" asks his mentor.

"You know how it is. Ever since I got promoted to corporate last year, I never get to see my wife and kids anymore. What I don't get is, now that I've hit all my goals and made a great career for myself, I feel empty—like I haven't accomplished much. It seems as though you've helped me make myself into a commodity, Roy, more than just a businessman."

"I'm glad to hear you say that," Roy replies with a smile.

"What, that I'm a commodity or that I need a vacation?" his pupil asks, obviously frustrated.

"Neither. You don't need a vacation, Oscar. What you need is a purpose."

"I have a purpose, remember? I need to create vision, fill quotas, and increase profits by quarter's end," Oscar says, exasperated.

"I've been waiting all these years for you to get to this point," his mentor says in a solemn voice. "I learned this lesson far too late in life, but you're in the right place at the right time to understand and actually enjoy what I'm about to share with you. Here," he says, handing his student a card.

I find it more enjoyable <u>investing</u> time in doing what pleases me, rather than <u>wasting</u> time inappropriately trying to please others...

"Oscar, if I gave you $10 million dollars today, would you quit working?" his advisor asks.

"Probably not," Oscar answers after a moment's thought, "but I would change what I do. I mean, I like the fact that I've worked my way up to vice president of the company. It was a great experience, but I think I'd take time to write if I had the chance."

"Exactly!" Roy exclaims, pointing his index finger at him. "You've hit the nail on the head. Most people, myself included, have a career or business that brings monetary gain but no sense of purpose. We get so caught up in the day-to-day actions and challenges of our lives that we rarely live up to our own potential. You can fulfill your potential only by focusing on and following your dream. That's where your purpose lies. Let me show you this," Roy says, pulling a chart out of his briefcase.

"This is a 'Flowchart of Success' I came up with," Roy tells Oscar, as the young man looks at the diagram. "Listen carefully," the older gentleman advises. Follow the illustration while I tell you the true secret for success on the job or in business and, more important, in life."

"Another secret? Gee, Roy, you've got a million of 'em!" Oscar teases his friend. "Go ahead and explain."

"Like you could stop me!" the older man says with a chuckle. "Okay, here goes. I believe everyone sits back, at least once in his or her life, and wonders, 'Why am I here? What is the master plan?' Guess who has that answer?"

"Me?" Oscar ventures.

"Of course! YOU and only YOU know what you are capable of and what you feel in your heart. Now let's look at how my flowchart works. See that arrow going up? It starts from 'fulfilling our basic needs,' because we are taught that is how life works.

"When we're young adults, moving out of the house for the first time, society and our families don't encourage us to go find our purpose. They expect us just to go out and get a job! This is so we can afford an apartment, transportation, food—in other words, fulfill our basic needs."

Roy stops to take a bite of his banana split.

FLOWCHART OF SUCCESS

- Finding Our Purpose and Focusing on It
- Feeling of Accomplishment
- Attaining Set Goals
- Setting Goals
- Affording Some Luxuries
- Wanting to Feel Appreciated
- Fulfilling Our Basic Needs

"And after we fulfill our basic needs, we start 'wanting to feel appreciated,'" Oscar comments, glancing at the second level on the diagram. "We might skip around from job to job or business to business—until we find one where we feel appreciated for what we have to offer, and we're getting paid what we're worth. Then we have a feeling of appreciation."

"Right," the mentor answers, wiping his mouth. "When we're finally making enough money, there's a little cash left over at the end of the month to put toward buying our first set of 'toys,' eating out more, getting massages, or maybe purchasing a fine new suit. That's called 'affording some luxuries.' You know, a bit of self-pampering."

"I like that part," Oscar comments with a grin.

"Yes, and you've already been there, done that. In fact, you've completed all the steps except the last. Still, I'm going to outline the others, because there's a natural progression I want you to see."

"Sure," Oscar says. "I'm listening."

"After we get a taste of the good life, we begin consciously setting goals for ourselves so we can have even more of the luxuries we've started to enjoy. We decide on a desired outcome, and then achieve it—like earning a promotion, starting a business, buying a new car, or even hitting a non-material target, such as losing weight or quitting smoking. This phase is called 'attaining set goals.'" When we've set a goal—say for a new car—saved up, worked hard, and applied ourselves toward that outcome, we feel great when we sign the deal in the showroom!"

"Yes!" Oscar exclaims. "That's where we get the 'feeling of accomplishment.'"

"Right," Roy replies. "It's the exhilaration of victory. Some call it the 'pink cloud syndrome.' But sadly, that's where the story usually ends. So many of us miss the most important life lesson of all, the true secret to our personal happiness and fulfillment, and that's...."

"Finding your purpose!" Oscar excitedly interrupts his mentor.

Roy smiles and nods. "Waking up each day knowing you make a difference. Never wasting even a moment worrying about what you do for a living, because when you're doing what you love—your passion—it's not work. It's your purpose, the reason you are here."

"Okay, I get that," Oscar says, "but how do you find your purpose?"

"Let me tell you a story about a young lady I met. She told me she'd just earned her master's degree in geriatrics, the study and care of the elderly. I asked her why she'd chosen that career, and she began to reel off statistics about the great starting salary, benefits, room for advancement, and so on and so forth. I thought to myself, 'She'll probably be successful. She seems like a real go-getter, but she'll probably only make her way up to step four, attaining set goals,'" Roy tells Oscar.

"Then, I asked the friend sitting beside the young lady what SHE wanted to do with her life. She told me she wanted to go into geriatrics too. I pressed for her reasons why. Her eyes lit up with joy, and she was off to the races. With great conviction, she told me about once having seen a documentary on retirement homes.

The film showed gruesome scenes of older people strapped to their beds, others vegetating in the halls in their wheelchairs, colostomy bags overflowing. She said she'd made a decision right then and there to do her best to help alleviate the shabby treatment and poor living conditions that exist in some retirement homes. She said she had elderly relatives in various homes across the country, and the thought of them living like that made her ill. She truly believed that if more young people entered the profession and took a stand, they could make a difference.

"'I'm going to be old myself someday,' she told me. 'I don't want to be warehoused until I die. Would you?' Then, with a warm smile, she added, 'Besides, there's no better feeling than to walk into the group area of a retirement home and see those grandmas and grandpas, widows and widowers brighten up at the prospect of company. All they want is someone to talk to, to make them feel young again, to make them feel alive!'"

"I'd say the second girl is starting at the top, right?" Oscar asks his mentor.

"Definitely," Roy says. "She's found her purpose. When she wakes up in the morning, she feels passion for what she is doing with her life. She feels it's what she was put on this planet to do! Now, look at the chart again. The arrow on the left is going down. That's because ALL the steps below will come naturally and more easily to those who've discovered their purpose."

"Tell me how that works," Oscar prompts.

"Okay," Roy agrees. "The gal who's found her purpose working in geriatrics will gain a feeling of accomplishment, because she's passionate about her work. She'll be thrilled that she's managed to get a good job in her chosen field. Her natural interest will motivate her to find ways to attain set goals to make a difference. She'll have luxuries because the job pays well, has good benefits, and a car allowance."

"Will she rise up in the company, do you think?" Oscar interrupts.

"Yes," the older man continues. "Her supervisor will promote her above the others, all other factors being equal, because of her passion for the work."

"Makes sense," Oscar pipes up.

"This breeds the feeling of appreciation," Roy notes. "Finally, the salary her starting position offers is enough to meet all her basic needs. She may even go on and flower into a geriatric-field entrepreneur, owning her own retirement home or homes!"

"Wow! It seems so simple...." Oscar murmurs thoughtfully, his head resting comfortably on his hand.

"Yes! It can and will be this easy once you've found what you truly want to do because..." Roy trails off as he hands his pupil another card.

When you do what you love, and love what you do, you'll have SUCCESS your whole life through.

"Ever wonder why 80 percent of college graduates don't go into the career for which they got their degrees?" Roy asks. "It's because most people are simply told to go to college, without being properly guided to study what truly INTERESTS them. They're told by society and their families of the great promise of certain careers—like medicine, accounting, law, and science—but they usually don't have any passion for them. They based their dreams on pleasing others rather than following their own hearts.

"Think of it like this," the mentor adds in response to Oscar's blank look. "Did Michael Jordan go to work at the arena every day or did he do what he enjoyed doing? Mother Teresa was an example of someone following her passion. The same goes for Tiger Woods, Peek-A-Boo Street, Bill Gates, Zig Ziglar, Oprah Winfrey, Rudy Giuliani, Tom Hanks, and Steven Spielberg, to name a few. They love what they do, and, YES, they work hard. But working at what you love to do is the best part of all!"

"But I don't have the kind of talent those people do," Oscar demurs doubtfully.

"That's not the point," Roy scolds. "The point is, each of these people found his or her purpose, and then pursued it with passion! Think of the feelings of appreciation and accomplishment they all must have. They attained and reached goals that surely seemed impossible at times. They know their basic needs will always be met, and they're amply rewarded with luxuries.

"But listen," the businessman continues patiently. "I'm not saying they didn't have to suffer and struggle along the way—and perhaps even go broke at some point. That's called paying your dues. Unless we are given or inherit a lot of money, we all need to go through that process anyway. So why not go through it pursuing your dream?"

"I see the difference," Oscar says. "It's one thing to be broke and struggling to meet your basic needs when you don't know where you're going. But it's something else entirely different to be broke when you *do* know where you're going. Say, for example, you're an actor. You do odd jobs, go to a lot of auditions, get parts, get turned down—all the while feeling you're paying your dues toward an outcome, toward your purpose!"

"That's the basic concept!" his good friend replies delightedly.

"But Roy, I'm too involved to change my career. Between bills and deadlines, I have a wife and two kids to think about. My life is too complicated. I can't change things now...."

"Can't change things?" Roy repeats. "Read this." And he hands his protégé another card.

Things are the way you THINK they are, because you THINK they are that way.

"Oscar," he says, lowering his voice, "it's like our quote from Henry Ford, 'If you think you can you're right; if you think you can't, you're right.' You're still a very young man, and you've had more success than many people will ever know in their entire lives. But to be truly happy in life—to wake up in the morning with a sense of purpose instead of just a deadline—you need to look within and follow your calling. You have plenty of time to change direction, but only you know which path is the best choice for you."

"But what about my family?" Oscar inquires. "Suppose my wife doesn't support my career change? What if I can't provide as well for my children?"

"Once you see things clearly, and take action in the direction of your objective," the aging man reassures him, "in all likelihood, you'll find that your wife will support you. Your children will continue to love you unconditionally. Everything, in that sense, will remain the same. It may even improve. Only your attitude of not just settling for an unsatisfactory career experience will change. You'll then take action toward something that excites you. I know you have enough of these cards to wallpaper your office, but here's another that sums this up so well."

Courageously step forward in faith, in spite of any fears. Your attitude is the main factor in your success or failure. So, make it a positive one!

"Here's an example of an attitude change—a different response to the same situation: You know how, when you're first in love, the other person seemingly can do no wrong?" Roy asks with a twinkle in his eye. "The way he or she spills a drink seems so cute. If that person accidentally bumps you on the head, you fall to the ground in each other's arms, laughing. Then about six months later, if he or she spills a drink, you may get irritated. Incredibly, you may even be blamed for the spill! Then, if your love accidentally bumps your head, you may think 'how clumsy,' right?"

"Right," Oscar says, laughing.

"What's changed? Same situation, same scenario, just a different perception. Everything in life is that way. If we leave the doctor's office after—God forbid—a health scare, life suddenly seems sweeter, doesn't it? The same goes for what we perceive as positive changes—when we get that new car, house, promotion and, oh yes, the big one, our first child is born. Remember how you were floating on cloud nine?"

"Yes," Oscar replies fondly. "That reminds me, I have some new photos of David and Celeste." The young man pulls out his wallet and the two take a short break so Roy can "ooh" and "aah" over Oscar's adorable children.

"But getting back to the lesson," Roy says sternly, as he hands the pictures back to Oscar, "the irony of the situation we were just talking about is when life *looks* different—but nothing may really be different at all! Your attitude just might have shifted for some other reason. Then, again, changes may have truly occurred. But it doesn't really matter, as long as we look for the good in everything as we go along, and change course as needed."

"Life is full of changes and opportunities. It's our attitude toward everything that's central to our success or failure, and therefore, our happiness. Right, Roy?"

"Right, my boy," beams the elderly gentleman. "Now, imagine a life where we are in a joyful state most of the time, where people are kinder, the flowers smell better, the birds sing more harmoniously, the sky is always blue, and yadda, yadda, yadda."

"Happy all the time, eh?" Oscar asks skeptically.

"Well, here's the good news!" Roy thunders back. "Life can be JUST LIKE THAT! All we have to do is CHOOSE! Know why? How about what it says on the card I just gave you?"

"Things are the way you think they are, because you think they are that way," Oscar answers with delight.

"At any given time, even getting knocked unconscious can seem romantic and fun—go figure," Roy responds playfully. "When someone gets under my skin or some situation is not to my liking, I tend to reflect on all the good things going on in my life. I know, at some deep level, that everything happens for a reason. Maybe certain individuals are upset, perhaps because they're feeling tired and stressed out. People usually have good intentions.

"More likely than not," Roy continues, with a smile, "I soon realize that the situation is not as grave as I had first thought. I just need to change my perspective on the matter—perhaps be more flexible and forgiving. Heaven knows, I have plenty of faults! Suppose I'd just won the lottery or hit that home run in the bottom of the ninth. Would I care as much about whatever situation was currently bothering me? You can see where this is headed, right?"

"There's always some light at the end of the tunnel," Oscar concurs. "So we need to focus on the light, look at the bright side of things. Give others the benefit of the doubt. You've taught me that, Roy."

"Good. I'm glad you see that the glass is always half full or half empty depending on your perspective. Overall, the level doesn't move much. What changes is the way we view the glass." Roy twirls his half-full water glass as he speaks.

"You know, Roy, now that I'm thinking of it, your triangle diagram of needs really hits home. It reminds me of Jeff, a guy I knew at corporate. He was a really nice guy, and he'd worked at the company for 30 years. His whole goal in life was to retire at 65, take his pension, and open a yogurt/ice cream shop, kind of like the one we're in now.

"Well, Jeff actually did it. He loved coming up with new flavors, and he dreamed that kids and grownups would come into his shop, chat a while, and call him Grandpa. As he pursued his vision, the people came—and they kept coming back. After only 18 months of Grandpa's so-called retirement, his daughter opened a second shop. Then his wife and two sisters opened another. Now they're up to 11 stores in all, and Grandpa Jeff is having the time of his life!"

"That's a great story," Roy comments.

"I thought so, too, but now you have my mind reeling," Oscar remarks. "What if my friend had opened that shop after only five years at corporate instead of 30? What if he'd acted as soon as he realized his purpose? How many shops would he have today, and how many more years could he have spent doing what he loves to do, instead of what he thought he 'should' do?"

Roy smiles slowly as he hands Oscar another card. "This is the last card I'll be sharing with you, Oscar. I've taught you all I can. Now, it's up to you to take this information and do with it what you choose."

As Oscar looks down at the card and reads it...

...he smiles at Roy. All at once, he knows he will fulfill his purpose.

"In the end, the extent of our own success will be measured by the accomplishments that we have helped create in others."

—Greg S. Reid

A Decade Later

Oscar's life has changed forever since his last regular meeting with Roy—ten years ago—the one where they talked about purpose. He gave up his corporate job to follow his dream of writing. Not only is Oscar now a bestselling novelist, he's opened his own publishing company to boot!

His books fly off the shelves in bookstores from coast to coast. His new career gives him more time to spend with his family, watching his children grow and flower. He and his wife and kids live very comfortably. Not only that, Oscar has met all the famous people he and Roy used to talk about throughout the years. And whenever possible, he's introduced his role model to them as well.

Although they no longer get together every month, the friends have kept in touch. Today, for old times' sake, they've agreed to meet again at the *Palace of Frozen Delights*.

"It seems you've become something of a celebrity," Roy teases, glancing at a couple in the booth nearby, whispering as they point in Oscar's direction.

"Loved your last book," Estelle tells Oscar as she puts down their coffee and the "usual"—a hot fudge sundae for him and a banana split for Roy. "But you could've written a bigger part for the crusty but lov-able ice-cream-shop server."

"Everybody's a critic," Oscar jokes.

"Only now you have to call me server/owner," Estelle tells them joyously, grinning from ear to ear. "You boys' positive vibes rubbed off on me. I convinced George to let me buy into the shop as his partner a couple years back. Then, when he finally retired, he just 'gave' his share to me for sticking around with him all this time. Bless his heart!"

"That's wonderful," Roy says warmly.

"Yes, congratulations!" Oscar chimes in. "This place must be magic or something!"

"Never lose sight of the magic," Roy says softly as Estelle moves away.

"I'll tell you, Roy," the young writer proceeds to compliment his friend, "I really need to hand it to you. Everything you taught me has really paid off. My publishing company runs itself nowadays, because I took your advice and empowered the right people to take care of things. I share the wealth with those who helped create it, and I use the lessons I learned at corporate to solve situations that arise from time to time. By the way, I have something for you."

Oscar reaches under the table and pulls out a storage box.

"What is it?" the mentor asks, eager as a boy.

"Open it and find out," Oscar tells him.

Roy lifts the top off the box and lets out a loud belly laugh. "You are a man of your word!" he exclaims, looking down at hundreds of tattered, old baseball cards. "Now we're even on the cards."

"Well, that's not all," Oscar says shyly. "I had something printed for you," and he hands a handsomely bound volume to his mentor. "It's a copy of every card you ever gave me," Oscar tells Roy, who is visibly moved, "along with commentary about your lessons and how much they've meant to me. I'm distributing this to bookstores all over the country. I'll donate the profits to whatever charity you name."

"A wonderful present, I must say." Roy pauses to dab at his eyes. "Allergies," he mutters. "Please give the baseball cards to your son for me, and donate the book's profits to the local mentoring program in each community where the book is sold. Thank you so much for thinking of me!"

"You've got it!" Oscar says with a gleeful, boyish grin. "And I have another surprise for you. As per our agreement when we began, I've decided the BEST way to share what you have taught me is to do it in the same fashion as you have done with me, so I have become a mentor. In fact my first mentee is due here in just a few minutes. "

The two men slowly exit the *Palace,* savoring each moment together, and hug one another goodbye. "Wait," Oscar calls as Roy starts to walk away. "Have I shown you my new car?" He gestures toward his shiny new Mercedes, much like a good game-show host, just as he'd shown off the bicycle of his dreams not so many years ago.

"That's a great choice, Oscar," congratulates Roy. "Good luck with your mentoring session," he shouts as he starts walking toward the corner. As his well-loved mentor reaches the curb, Roy pauses for a moment and then turns around when he hears a small voice pipe up from behind.

A boy, no older than Oscar was when he and Roy met, looks up at Oscar and says the now-familiar words, "Wow, is that your car? You must be rich! How did you get that way?"

Roy's heart swells with joy, as he watches Oscar lean down to the boy. Oscar reaches into his vest pocket, and hands the lad the same card Roy had given to *him* at *their* first meeting. It reads, "Dreams are realities on which you haven't yet taken ACTION." Oscar then says to the boy, "It looks as though we have a situation here.

"What do you mean?" the lad asks, looking a little alarmed.

"Well, we could either stand outside this ice cream shop talking business, or we could go inside and continue over a sundae…"

—Now It's Your Turn—

Share Roy's "Famous" Success Cards with Others
Please feel free to copy and share Roy's cards with others.
They are duplicated on pages 101 through 108
for your copying convenience.

Roy's "Famous" Success Cards

Dreams are realities on
which you haven't yet
taken ACTION.

From The Millionaire Mentor by Greg S. Reid, Published by Possibility Press

NEVER GIVE UP!
The only two times you
need to keep pushing
on are:
When you want to and when you don't!

From The Millionaire Mentor by Greg S. Reid, Published by Possibility Press

Our most valuable
possession is the
one that possesses
us to share.

From The Millionaire Mentor by Greg S. Reid, Published by Possibility Press

Before you can even hope
to reach a goal, you first
need to HAVE one.

From The Millionaire Mentor by Greg S. Reid, Published by Possibility Press

Our success is most assured when we duplicate our efforts by leveraging with others.

From The Millionaire Mentor by Greg S. Reid, Published by Possibility Press

The difference between just TRYING to do something and actually DOING it is found in the OUTCOME.

From The Millionaire Mentor by Greg S. Reid, Published by Possibility Press

It's as easy as A.B.C.— Always Be Closing

From The Millionaire Mentor by Greg S. Reid, Published by Possibility Press

The fear of loss outweighs the benefit of gain.

From The Millionaire Mentor by Greg S. Reid, Published by Possibility Press

Sell Situation→Situation Sells
Sell Emotion→Emotion Sells

When you have an
EMOTIONAL SITUATION,
you'll have yourself a SALE.

From The Millionaire Mentor by Greg S. Reid, Published by Possibility Press

---

<u>The most effective steps to a close</u>:

STEP 1→Contact the decisionmaker
STEP 2→Qualify and warm up
STEP 3→Present
STEP 4→Close
STEP 5→Warm down

From The Millionaire Mentor by Greg S. Reid, Published by Possibility Press

---

You CAN do it.
You WILL do it.
Just Shuck Another Oyster!

From The Millionaire Mentor by Greg S. Reid, Published by Possibility Press

---

Tell them what they
NEED to hear, not what
they WANT to hear.

From The Millionaire Mentor by Greg S. Reid, Published by Possibility Press

I feel so good—
even I want
to be me.

From The Millionaire Mentor by Greg S. Reid, Published by Possibility Press

To get what YOU
want, you FIRST need
to help others get
what THEY want!

From The Millionaire Mentor by Greg S. Reid, Published by Possibility Press

A DREAM written down with a
date becomes a GOAL. A goal
broken down becomes a PLAN.
A plan backed by ACTION makes
your dream come true.

From The Millionaire Mentor by Greg S. Reid, Published by Possibility Press

The true measure of a
person's integrity is the
extent to which he or
she is accountable.

From The Millionaire Mentor by Greg S. Reid, Published by Possibility Press

LEADERS create the vision, set the example, and empower others to help make it happen.

From The Millionaire Mentor by Greg S. Reid, Published by Possibility Press

Share ideas and information generously.

From The Millionaire Mentor by Greg S. Reid, Published by Possibility Press

The true measure of all great leaders is how well they weather the storms.

From The Millionaire Mentor by Greg S. Reid, Published by Possibility Press

We learn more about the character of people on one OFF day, than on all their ON days put together.

From The Millionaire Mentor by Greg S. Reid, Published by Possibility Press

Avoid people
who have negative
attitudes.

From The Millionaire Mentor by Greg S. Reid, Published by Possibility Press

There is nothing as
POWERFUL as a
POSITIVE ATTITUDE.

From The Millionaire Mentor by Greg S. Reid, Published by Possibility Press

GIVE
BACK

From The Millionaire Mentor by Greg S. Reid, Published by Possibility Press

EMPOWER
through
DELEGATION

From The Millionaire Mentor by Greg S. Reid, Published by Possibility Press

 **What is important is how well we perform a task, not how big it is.**

From The Millionaire Mentor by Greg S. Reid, Published by Possibility Press

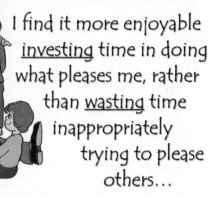 **I find it more enjoyable <u>investing</u> time in doing what pleases me, rather than <u>wasting</u> time inappropriately trying to please others…**

From The Millionaire Mentor by Greg S. Reid, Published by Possibility Press

When you do what you love, and love what you do, you'll have SUCCESS your whole life through.

From The Millionaire Mentor by Greg S. Reid, Published by Possibility Press

Things are the way you THINK they are, because you THINK they are that way.

From The Millionaire Mentor by Greg S. Reid, Published by Possibility Press

Courageously step forward in faith, in spite of any fears. Your attitude is the main factor in your success or failure.
So, make it a positive one!

From The Millionaire Mentor by Greg S. Reid, Published by Possibility Press

All I want in life is to give my life my all.

From The Millionaire Mentor by Greg S. Reid, Published by Possibility Press

"The truly rich have hearts of gold."

—Greg S. Reid

Who Is Greg Reid?

Greg Reid is founder of Work$mart, Inc., an advertising/promotional company in San Diego, California. *The Millionaire Mentor* is his first book. His more than twenty years of sales and marketing experience is distilled into this drama, which is based on real-life, hard-won lessons, and achieving true success.

Like his character Roy, in the book, he believes in giving back. Greg teaches that we can achieve anything in life as long as we believe in ourselves, focus on our goals, and help others.

When he speaks at businesses, charity events, universities, and other venues, Greg demonstrates that determination, backed by a positive attitude, can work wonders. He is living proof that this philosophy works.